Soulful Writings

Reflections of a Young Poet's Imagination

MAHIR VASUDEV

Made with ❤ on the Notion Press Platform

www.notionpress.com

To my family, teachers, pals and my dad for encouraging me to pen down my thoughts.

Contents

Preface

From writing simplistic verses just to match rhymes, to spending almost a year for my poems such as Christmastime, my journey with poetry has been transformative.

It all traces back to the year 2019. My family and I had recently come back from an exhilarating experience in Turkey. Inspired by my father's poetic retelling of our trip, 'Beautiful Turkey', I embraced writing as both a hobby and a passion. Initially my writings were whimsical, until 2020. For promoting environmentalism, I wrote **'Trees Gone by'**. Since then, my love for the power of words kept accruing.

I penned down my thoughts on several occasions, including the moments of sorrow, joyousness, love, and excitement. This book also consists of poems written by my dad that inspired me to write and never let my inner author die.

In this book, you shall traverse through the hallway of four years of me as an author, wherein you will be going through a ridiculously diverse palate of emotions, from profound love for family, to the stark realities of the world. Poems after ***'Escaping Darkness'*** are written by my dad.

Mahir Vasudev | March 2024
thisismahir007@gmail.com

Acknowledgments

I express deep gratitude to my wonderful parents, whose encouragement has been the cornerstone of my writing endeavors. Heartfelt thanks to my grandparents for their wisdom and love, shaping my perspective through the years. A special appreciation for my dedicated teachers who emphasized the significance of reading and helped enhance my vocabulary. A heartfelt shout-out to my Mami[1], whose guidance during creative roadblocks and assistance in finding the right words enriched my poems.

Lastly, nature, a constant companion, has influenced my writing, adding depth and beauty to my words.

This acknowledgment doesn't mark the end, but a new beginning to write more and articulate my thoughts.

---

[1] Aunt

1. Trees Gone By

Loitering in the woods,
Watching stags eat grass as much as they could.

Eagles' eyries on the tress,
Feeding eaglets one, two and three.

As soon as the rain arrives,
Beautiful lichens grow and rise.

Suddenly, I wake up as the mosquito bites,
Just to realise it was a beautiful dream in disguise.

It's all concrete jungle left,
While birds find a tree for a nest.

No more grass for stags to eat,
Trees are gone and now it's only the scorching
heat.

2. Entering The Gate Of A New Day

Waking up during the dawn,
With a loud yawn.

The early morning jog,
For the laziness cure,

The sun's shades orange, blue and yellow,
Saying 'Good Morning' to all my congenial fellows.

The beautiful weather that makes you feel as light as a feather,
Enjoying yourself with your family together.

The glistening sun reflects the water waves,
And makes you wait there for days.

As the sun sets into the sea with the shadows of gorgeous coconut trees,
And the animals go back to their home just like the alluring birds, cuckoo, crows and geese.

As the moon awaits,
I get ready to enter the gate of a new day.

3. Mom and Dad

You're the most benevolent and wonderful people in this universe,
Staying without you feels no better than living with a curse.

I have traversed through the hallway of your love for me,
And learnt that we have a connection like the waves and the sea.

Thank you for everything you have done for me,
Whenever I hurt you, I feel as if I am surrounded by the evil and dreadful black sea.

You are my world, you are my light,
You have given me might and the finest and greatest life.

4. My Parents, My Pride

Today, I shall take a moment to thank God for the parents he has bestowed upon me,
Your presence is the only thing required for my face to light up with glee.

I have always felt culpable for each time I have hurt your feelings,
Thou art my inspiration, thou art my dearest, thou art my favourite beloved beings.

I can't bear to see you apart,
I hope our love's ways, not even in after life, ever part.

You have always stood by my side whenever I needed you,
Our bond continues to grow stronger and stronger just like our love accrues.

You have always managed to find a ray of light in my life whenever I was in pain,
I love you to the moon, and back again.

5. Love you

Looking at you makes me want to get wrapped
around your shoulders,
Whenever I fell, you held me like a holder.

I am the sword and you are the hilt,
Whenever I hurt you, I feel a sense of guilt.

You are so kind, I wonder how you read my mind,
The shine on your face makes me go blind.

I am grateful for having parents like you,
Thank you for everything you do.

6. Can't Thank Enough

Sometimes,
I wonder whether if I'm grateful enough to my father,
For helping me enter the room full of happiness, through a small embrasure.

Sometimes,
I wonder whether if I am thankful enough to my father,
For making a new chapter in my life full of happiness on the miserable chapters' erasure.

Sometimes,
I wonder whether if I am appreciative enough to my father,
For consoling my irritation and anger.

You are not only a father but a friend, a bro, an emotion,
I love you more than the water in the ocean.

7. My Guiding Light

It's bewildering how you manage to keep me gleeful and contented at all times,
Hearing your voice after you return home, is as pleasing as ringing chimes.

You're the one who has held my hand since birth,
You are the main pillar of my life, the main reason of my mirth.

I ponder where my happiness would have faded without you,
Whenever I was stuck in any strife, you would be my guiding hand all the way through.

It's you, my source of entertainment, my source of light and my helping hand,
Our bonds continue to grow stronger and our love continues to expand.

I'm grateful for all the love you have showered on me,
Thank you for the care, thank you for the precious gifts, and the life you have let me live a-free.

8. My Grandpa

*They say, grandpas are people who have silver hair
and a golden heart,
Whenever I feel low, you're the first to give my
mood a fresh start.*

*They say, when one embraces their grandpa, they
feel a sense of richness, as though they're on cloud
nine,
To me, your love is as rich as a gold mine.*

*They say, a grandpa and a grandchild share their
thoughts and fantasies everyday,
When we take a seat by each other, we never run
short of thing to say.*

*They say, a grandpa, with every touch, brings
wisdom, warmth and love,
A person like you is sent from angels above.*

*For me, he's my love, the light of my life,
I wonder what I would've done without thou my
best friend, I pray, you never depart to afterlife.*

9. Grandparents

You'll are the most special people on Earth,
Spending time with you is the cause of my mirth.

You'll have supported me through thick and thin,
Just a glimpse of you makes me grin.

Your personality is as good as gold,
I hope that you always keep glowing and never get old.

You will always shine in my heart,
Come what may, we will never be set apart.

10. The Love Of My Life

The love of my life is someone I truly love, care for, and adore,
Without her, my life would be lonely as a corpse.

The love of my life is someone I truly love, care for, and adore,
It was she who brought along a flood of light in my life, by revealing a new door.

The love of my life is someone I truly love, care for, and adore,
Her face, her personality, her smile makes me want to love her more and more.

The love of my life is someone I truly love, care for, and adore,
My love for her keeps increasing as fast as a lightning bolt.

She is indispensable to me just like the sun is to the plant,
She is my love, she is my life, she is my aunt.

11. My Affectionate Pal

It's been a while since I last thanked you for
supporting me and always having my back,
I'm blessed to have thee, a person with a heavy
knowledge sack.

It's been a while since I last apologised for the
arguments we've had,
Thou art the one who has been successful in
uplifting my mood whenever I was unhappy and
sad.

It's been a while since I last said I'm grateful to you
for teaching me valuable aspects of life,
You've helped me find my way through, in any kind
of strife.

Lastly, I am indebted to you for the exhilarating
moments you have let me live a-free,
I ponder how I will repay thee with all the love
you've showered on me.

12. Stay With Me

Stay with me,
As I will need your help to escape this world full of misery.

Stay with me,
As need someone, to talk to, love, and believe.

Stay with me,

As the only person who has my back, is my first and last priority.

Stay with me,
And help me break free of this traumatic world, with such ease.

I hope to see my self high in the sky soon,
But that can only happen with your help, that gets me higher and higher, closer to the moon.

But one day we all have to go,
So why not keep hopes, and do our utmost.
You're the only spirit, the only heart I know,

Let us show the world, that we can fly higher than the vultures, eagles and the mighty Condor.

You're the lone soul I see in my life,
You're my only love, you're my only light.

13. Mother

Mother,
You're the one who has helped me be the master of my circumstances,
And cause my pain to smother.

Mother,
We live on a land full of cruelty,
But you have helped me through, with no difficulties.

Mother,
You're the one who has brought into my life peace,
You have helped me sail through my problems, with such ease.

Mother,
It's you, my guiding light, my happiness, my love, my life,
Your love for me and my love for you is unconditional and rife.

14. Farewell

You came as little children crying and wailing,
Opportunities came your way through which you were sailing.

You failed and you cried,
We were proud and happy whenever you tried.

It's sad to see you all leave this day,
But we know our army is prepared, come what may.

May you all have a successful and a happy life ahead,
And win over things that you always used to dread.

Our wishes are with you to reach where you wish to,
We all love you!

15. Freedom

It feels so beautiful to be liberated,
Always free and not gated.

But there was a time when life was so painful,
The Brits made our life shameful.

We were abused and suppressed,
Our demands were all rejected and never addressed.

It was so difficult living during those times,
Every night we prayed that our pain sublimes.

Years went by and the outsiders exploited us,
We fought, we failed, but still had the guts.

We were tortured and we cried,
But we were happy that we at least tried.

During the 1947 monsoons,
India experienced spring when the nation bloomed.

The clouds of darkness fell on the British empire,
It was a sign for us to ascend higher.

Freedom has given us a reason to rejoice,
We can do what we want out of our own choice.

Freedom has helped us to aspire high,
It has given us the right to question why.

But we all must remember that freedom has come at a price,
It's only because of our freedom fighters and loved one's sacrifice.

Always be united and stay one,
To reap the benefits of freedom and enjoy the morning sun.

16. Happiness

As I opened the curtains the sun glistened on me,
I looked at the little birds enjoying above the shade-loving trees.

I asked the birds if they wanted something to eat,
They said yes and thanked me for the treat.

Soon I saw more birds come for the treat so I kept outside a box of grains,
Suddenly came the rain and all of it was in vain.

I looked up at the menacing but beautiful looking sky,
And let out a shrill cry.

I blamed myself for not living a materialistic life even though I had my druthers,
But then I realised, happiness exists in helping others.

17. Christmastime

It's that day of the year, when joy and exhilaration set foot into our lives,
It adds one more to our rich memories' archive.

It's that day of the year, when bells ring and carols play,
The emotion so called sadness, gets taken away.

It's that day of the year when you live your life to the fullest,
The warmth and togetherness of this occasion brightens the dullest.

We guffaw on this day, we make merry on this day,
We unravel the way to happiness' gateway.

It's the day when you feel a sense of bliss, delight and richness,
It's the greatest occasion of the year, it's the occasion of Christmas.

We embellish our homes and Christmas trees,
We spread love, kindness and spend time with our friends and families.

We wait for Santa to depart with all the gifts from Lapland,
And his reindeers to start flying at his command.

We get thrilled as Santa gets ready with bags full of gifts on his sleigh,
And deliver gifts all along the way.

Sadly, the excitement has started to go down with work on everyone's hands,
Let's revive the festival and make Santa feel our love for him and Christmas, before he lands.

18. Escaping Darkness

I am stuck in this cage of darkness,
All I need to escape is a bit of helpfulness.

I am stuck in this cage of darkness,
I am unable to escape because this world is full of curtness.

I am stuck in this cage of darkness,
This world is full of arguments and situations of absurdness.

I hope to see some bright light to escape this dreadful aspect of life,
Living life like this feels like being stabbed with a knife.

I dream of a life of joy and happiness,
But life in this world is full of ghastliness.

I pray to God for a better life,
I wonder what he will do to a human living a lowlife.

19. Beautiful Turkey

The Balloons rides,
Up in the skies.

Deep dark caves,
Look like lovely waves.

Pigeon holes with wind so cold,
In your arms I want to fold.

Fairy chimneys up so high,
Feels like kissing skies.

Rose valleys, mountain hills,
It's the beautiful cold chills.

Wish I could stay and spend more time,
But it's time to bid good bye.

20. Winds Of Change

I am amazed that things change so fast,
Like a river that was frozen in the past,
Has now devastated a beautiful town,
And has completely brought it down.

The calm and pleasant winds have gone,
And it has taken over by the mighty storm.

The fire that was once used to light up the house,
Has burnt and destroyed the homes of many while they were asleep,
And now the child just sits in the corner every day to weep.

I know that things don't stay the same,
It's time for every one to change.

I always look at change as a breath of fresh air,
But this time it's just not fair.

It just feels like we met you yesterday,
Wasn't it too soon to know it was your last day?

Guess that was destiny, all good times come to an end,
Let me not dwell the past and try things to mend.

What has gone is gone,
These were the winds of change,
And it will now spread its fragrance of love and care at a new place again.

21. Water Wings

Months have gone by and the wait is over,
Strong winds are seen coming after a long composure.

The winds are the sign of delight,
It's time for the beautiful rains to show their sight.

Grief, sorrows and pain are all set to go,
Of the farmer who waited for the rainy winds to blow.

The peacocks have started dancing with joy,
It's that time of the year that is full of fun, relief and for almost every one to enjoy.

While the rain gives many of us relief,
There are also times when it brings a lot of grief.

The little boy who enjoyed with his paper boat,
Now is stranded in a flooded village with very little hope.

The city that never slept, was young and always on fire,
Is now calm, silent, flooded, and seems to retire.

The people now again begin the wait,
The rains and the winds that they once loved is now the only thing that they hate.

Rain is like birds with wings,
As the season's over, their next journey begins,
To heal another dry land,
Cool the winds and wet the sand.

22. Out Of Darkness

The silence of the night,
Brings back all the chills and the fright.

In this deep darkness my mind goes blind,
Nothing to remember that were left behind.

I don't want to start seeing things in false light,
As then I feel to have started losing this fight.

I gently close my eyes,
For the blissful dreams to arise.

To take me to a land with joy, love and hope,
Hatred and sorrow, for you there is no scope.

As my beautiful dreams come to an end,
The dark night, its time for you to descend.

Beautiful day has come to take your place,
Fresh feelings, rigor is all that I will embrace.

It's now time for me to live with love, joy and no pain,
To make my dream a reality once again.

23. Keep Walking

Do not fear silence,
As silence brings in peace,
It's calm like a sea,
And you can hear the speaking tree.

The dark stary nights,
And the subtle movement of air,
That's all we need today in this world of despair.

The silence of the white winter nights,
Or the view into the valley from great heights,
Is all that we need,
And will calm us down indeed.

Things have not been good so far,
City has chaos, fear and negativity as a scar.

It's time to be patient and calm,
And in just a matter of time,
You will see the dawn that will spread like a
beautiful flowery vine.

24. Winter

Always dreamt of a cold winter day,
Me cuddled in my bed like a rabbit tucked in hay.

My dream turns to be true,
As this month the city's temperature is apt for a cup of hot stew.

It's time to light a bonfire tonight,
Sit around it and enjoy the dark starry sight.

As the cold subtle wind breezes through,
There are goosebumps being felt on you.

Let me quickly wrap you around,
To feel the same coziness and our lost love to rebound.

In this cold winter night I hear no sound,
As we sit in front of the the bonfire quietly on the ground.

I can feel your heart beat to the tune of our love,
With beautiful stars in the sky above.

25. My Soulmate

Once again comes the beautiful stary night,
Like always this time too I want to see you in my sight.

You are my strength and you are my confidence,
You are my companion in true sense.

Your beautiful eyes full for light and hope,
Memories full of joy and happiness are in my heart's envelope.

Your perfect smile, captures the hearts of a million who see you,
But I know it's only for me, like you say, 'from me to you.'

Your heart so warm and full of love,
A deep soul, full of affection like beautiful turtle dove.

Glossary

Trees Gone By

Loitering: to stand or walk around somewhere for no obvious reason.

Stags: the male of a deer.

Eyries: a large nest of an eagle or other bird of prey, built high in a tree or on a cliff.

Lichens: a grey, green, or yellow plant-like organism that grows on rocks, walls, and trees.

Entering the Gates of a New Day

Congenial: (of a person) pleasing or liked on account of having qualities or interests that are similar to one's own.

Glistening: to shine.

Mom and Dad

Benevolent: kind, friendly and helpful to others.

Traversed: to cross or travel through an area of land or water.

My Parents, My Pride

Bestowed: to give something to somebody, especially to show how much he/she is respected

Culpable: responsible for something bad that has happened.

thou art: you are.

Can't Thank Enough

Embrasure: An opening.

Erasure: the removal of writing, recorded material, or data.

My Guiding Light

Bewildering: confusing and difficult to understand.

Gleeful: happy, excited, or pleased.

Mirth: amusement or laughter.

The Love Of My Life

Corpse: a dead body, especially of a person.

My Affectionate Pal

Strife: trouble or fighting between people or groups.

Exhilarating: causing strong feelings of happy excitement and elation.

Stay With Me

Condor: a type of vulture.

Mother

Smother: to kill somebody by covering his/her face so that he/she cannot breathe.

Farewell

Wailing: to cry or complain in a loud, high voice, especially because you are sad or in pain.

Happiness

Menacing: threatening.

Water Wings

Composure: the state of being calm and having your feelings under control.

Keep Walking

Despair: the state of having lost all hope.

www.ingramcontent.com/pod-product-compliance
Lightning Source LLC
LaVergne TN
LVHW041257150826
845673LV00008B/2631
* 9 7 9 8 8 9 3 2 2 5 4 5 7 *